Anacondas
Nature's Biggest Snake

Taylor Fenmore

Lerner Publications ◆ Minneapolis

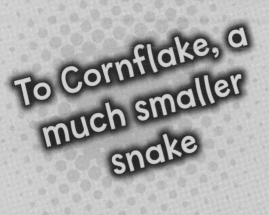

To Cornflake, a much smaller snake

Lerner Publications Company
An imprint of Lerner Publishing Group, Inc.
241 First Avenue North
Minneapolis, MN 55401 USA

For reading levels and more information, look up this title at www.lernerbooks.com.

Main body text set in Billy Infant Regular. Typeface provided by SparkType.

Editor: Brianna Kaiser **Designer:** Martha Kranes

Library of Congress Cataloging-in-Publication Data

Names: Fenmore, Taylor, author.
Title: Anacondas : nature's biggest snake / Taylor Fenmore.
Description: Minneapolis : Lerner Publications, [2024] | Series: Lightning Bolt books - nature's most massive animals | Includes bibliographical references and index. | Audience: Ages 6-9 | Audience: Grades 2-3 | Summary: "Anacondas are apex predators, and green anacondas are the heaviest snakes in the world. Readers will love learning all about the lives of these massive animals, including where they live and the prey they eat"— Provided by publisher.
Identifiers: LCCN 2023005562 (print) | LCCN 2023005563 (ebook) | ISBN 9798765608388 (library binding) | ISBN 9798765615263 (epub)
Subjects: LCSH: Anaconda—Juvenile literature. | BISAC: JUVENILE NONFICTION / Animals / Reptiles & Amphibians
Classification: LCC QL666.O63 F46 2024 (print) | LCC QL666.O63 (ebook) | DDC 597.96/7—dc23/eng/20230206

LC record available at https://lccn.loc.gov/2023005562
LC ebook record available at https://lccn.loc.gov/2023005563

Manufactured in the United States of America
1-1009283-51492-3/10/2023

Table of Contents

Meet the Anaconda

A hungry anaconda sees a caiman. The snake whips its head forward to strike at its meal. Then the snake coils tightly around it.

Green anacondas are the world's heaviest snakes. They can weigh more than 550 pounds (249 kg).

An anaconda slithers on the ground in Brazil.

Growing Up

Baby anacondas are about 2 feet (0.6 m) long at birth. They can swim, slither, and hunt right away. They quickly leave their mother.

Females are bigger than males. Females can grow up to 30 feet (9 m) long and 1 foot (0.3 m) around.

Anacondas reach their full size in about three to four years.

Eating prey helps anacondas grow big. Young snakes eat smaller prey such as fish and small mammals. Adult snakes eat bigger prey such as deer, caimans, and turtles.

An anaconda eats a wood stork, a kind of bird.

Anacondas are not active hunters. Instead, they hide and wait for prey to come by.

Anacondas of all ages eat prey.

Hidden Hunters

Anacondas live mainly in tropical rain forests in South America. They spend most of their time in water such as marshes or streams.

Anacondas can stay underwater to hide from prey. Anacondas can see and breathe while in the water because their eyes and noses are on top of their heads.

Anacondas can move faster in water than on land.

Anacondas also spend time on land. They rest on riverbanks and in trees where they can quickly reach the water if needed.

An anaconda resting on a tree

Their coloring helps them blend in. Their skin is green or brown with dark spots. They have yellow-and-black bellies.

Blending in with surroundings helps anacondas hide from prey.

Top predators like anacondas are called apex predators.

Because of their size, anacondas are top predators. No other animal preys on them. But if they feel threatened, they might rear back to prepare to strike.

Their senses detect prey and threats. They can detect chemicals from other animals by flicking their tongues.

Anacondas have heat-sensing pits on their lips.

Large Lives

Anacondas live about ten years in the wild. Anacondas are also in zoos or kept as pets. Those snakes sometimes live more than twenty years.

Snakes mate to produce babies.

Anacondas live alone. They have their own hunting areas and usually stay within them. But adults come together in late spring to mate.

A group of five-day-old anacondas

Female anacondas do not lay eggs. They give birth to twenty to forty live babies. They mate and give birth every other year.

The baby snakes help continue the life cycle. Anacondas start small but have a big life ahead.

Some anacondas grow up in zoos.

Anaconda Diagram

nostril

eye

scales

jaw

Fun Facts

- Anacondas only need to eat every few weeks. But after mating, a female may not eat for up to seven months while babies grow inside her.

- Anacondas have four rows of teeth on their upper jaws to help them catch and hold prey.

- A group of anacondas is called a bed or a knot.

Glossary

caiman: a small reptile from Central and South America that's related to and looks like an alligator

cycle: the different stages of something, such as a snake's life

detect: to notice or discover

mammal: a warm-blooded animal that feeds its young with milk and is covered in hair or fur

marsh: an area of soft, wet land usually overgrown by plants such as grasses

mate: to pair for breeding

predator: an animal that gets food mostly by killing and eating other animals

prey: an animal that is hunted or killed by another animal for food

Learn More

Anaconda Facts for Kids
https://kids.kiddle.co/Anaconda

Anaconda: Super Squeezers
https://sdzwildlifeexplorers.org/animals/anaconda

Boutland, Craig. *Green Anaconda*. Minneapolis: Bearport, 2021.

Davies, Monika. *Deadly Anacondas*. New York: Gareth Stevens, 2023.

Humphrey, Natalie. *Anaconda: The Largest Snake on Earth*. New York: Enslow, 2021.

National Geographic Kids: Anaconda
https://kids.nationalgeographic.com/animals/reptiles/facts/anaconda

Index

Photo Acknowledgments

Image credits: Wirestock, Inc./Alamy Stock Photo, p. 4; FernandoQuevedo/Getty Images, p. 5; PUMPZA/Shutterstock, p. 6; Juergen Ritterbach/Alamy Stock Photo, p. 7; slowmotiongli/ Getty Images, pp. 8, 14; Martin Harvey/Getty Images, p. 9; Mark Newman/Getty Images, p. 10; MattiaATH/Getty Images, p. 11; Luis Espin/Getty Images, pp. 12, 17; Andrew Clark/ Getty Images, p. 13; RMMPPhotography/Shutterstock, p. 15; Danny Ye/Shutterstock, p. 16; REUTERS/Alamy Stock Photo, pp. 18, 19; Sofiia Potanina/Alamy Stock Photo, p. 20.

Cover: Imagebroker/Alamy Stock Photo.